The Sandwich that Jack Made

Story by Elspeth Graham
Pictures by Chris Mould

OXFORD
UNIVERSITY PRESS

Jack found some butter.

Then he found some bread.

2

Here is the butter he spread on the bread.

Then he found some tomatoes,

all juicy and red.

Here are the tomatoes, all juicy and red,

on top of the butter he spread on the bread.

Then Jack found some rice,

and a big jar of spice.

Jack put in some rice and added some spice.

Here is the rice, covered in spice.
It's on the tomatoes, all juicy and red,
on top of the butter Jack spread on the bread.

Then Jack found some chips
and a packet of dips.

He mixed up the dips
and added the chips.

Here are the chips, mixed with the dips.
They went on the rice, covered in spice,
over tomatoes, juicy and red,

on top of the butter he spread on the bread.

16

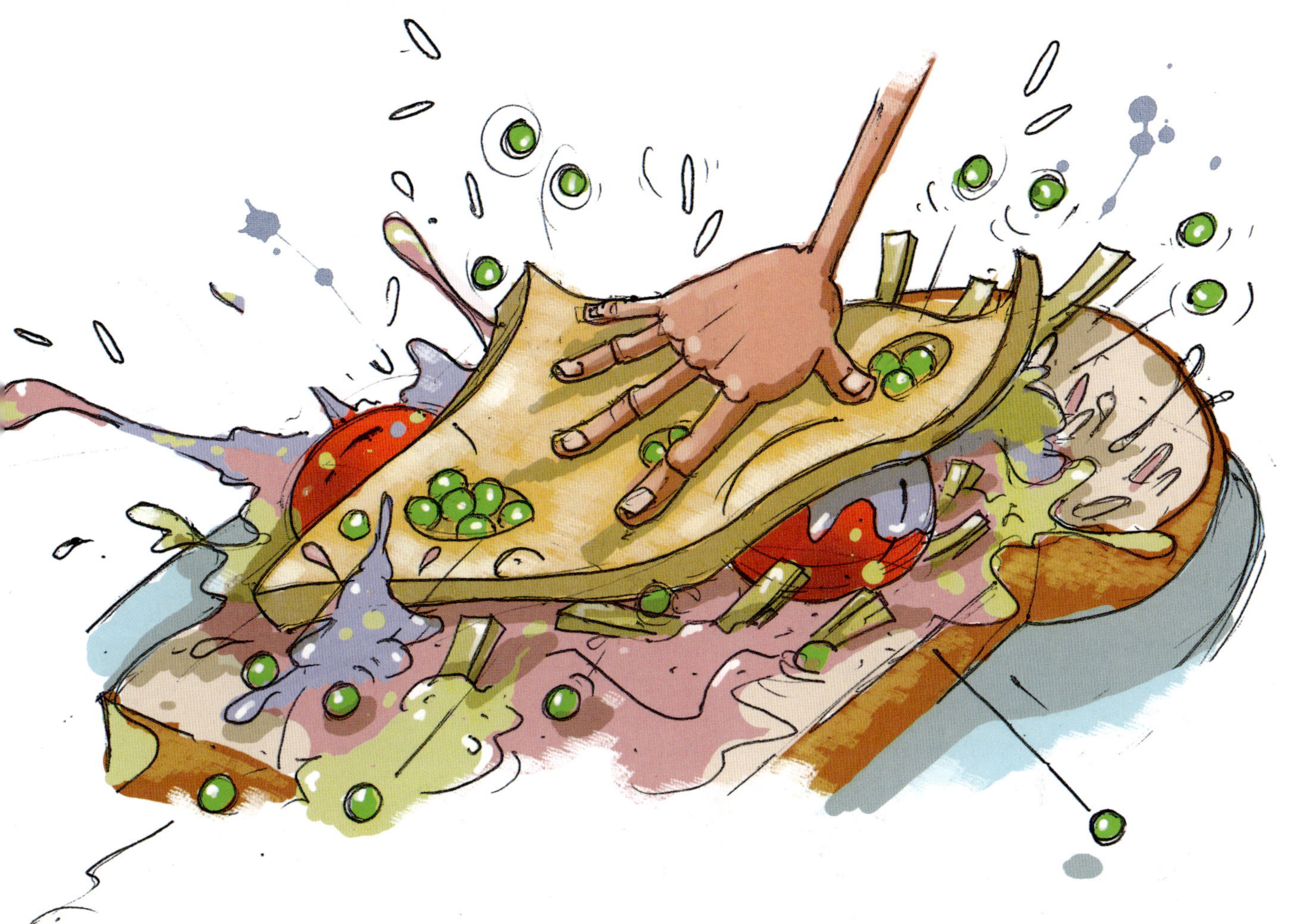

He added the peas and some of the cheese.

Here are the peas with some of the cheese.

They went on the chips, mixed with the dips,

on top of the rice, covered with spice,

over tomatoes, juicy and red,

on top of the butter Jack spread on the bread.

Then Jack found a pot of thick yellow cream.
He found a big lettuce, crispy and green.
He covered it all with the thick yellow cream.

Here is the lettuce, crispy and green,
dripping with lots of the thick yellow cream.
Jack put it on top of the cheese and green peas,

over the chips mixed with the dips,
on top of the rice, covered in spice,
over tomatoes, juicy and red,
on top of the butter he spread on the bread.

Jack took some more bread, nice and thick.
He put it on top...

... but then he felt sick!